Submerged

Submerged

John Findura

Five Oaks Press
FIVE-OAKS-PRESS.COM

Copyright ©2017 John Findura
All rights reserved. First print edition.

Five Oaks Press
Newburgh, NY 12550
five-oaks-press.com
editor@five-oaks-press.com

Cover Art and Author Photo: John R. Findura, Sr

ISBN: 978-1-944355-37-1

Printed in the United States of America

Acknowledgements

Columbia: A Journal of Literature and Art: "I Never Thought I'd See What I Saw," "It Will Be Different," "Something Happened," "The Ocean Is In The Road," and "There Are Boats In The Street Five Blocks From The Ocean"

Vinyl: "Bikini/Good Question"

A very heartfelt "Thank You!" to the following family, friends, and teachers who have helped me along the way: John & Janice Findura, Michael, Kim & Ethan Findura, Kristen, Jordan & Taylor Leck, Richard Findura, Jerry & Lynda Van De Polder, Timothy Liu, David Shapiro, Brad Gooch, David Lehman, Robert Polito, Elaine Equi, Mark Bibbins, Prageeta Sharma, Laurie Sheck, Tom Sleigh, Brian Russell, Billy Collins, Brian Simoneau, Anna & O.J. Guzon, Margaret Maria Roidi, Sander Zulauf, everyone at The Bread Loaf Writers' Conference & The Key West Literary Seminar, Lynn Houston and Five Oaks Press for rescuing me, little Sadie pup, and most importantly, Lauren, Hailey & Chloe Findura.

Contents

The Sea / Bikini	7
Thoughts About Water	8
A Bigger Boat	9
Teeth	10
I Never Thought I'd See What I Saw Today	11
A Bigger Boat	12
The Water Speaks / I Am Furious	13
Submerged / The Water	14
A Bigger Boat	15
Submerged / Library	16
A Bigger Boat	17
Things That The Water Took	18
The Water Speaks / The Taste	20
The Bikini / The Water	21
It Will Be Different	22
A Bigger Boat	23
Submerged / A Small Book	24
A Bigger Boat	25
The Water Speaks / You Can Run	26
I Do Not Like This	27
A Bigger Boat	28
The Hudson River Came	29
Submerged / Photo In A Barn	30
A Bigger Boat	31

Stay Pure	32
Submerged / You Look Perfect	33
A Bigger Boat	34
Submerged / Singing	35
Something Happened	36
A Bigger Boat	37
I See That A New Lake Has Formed	38
Submerged / Manhattan	39
A Bigger Boat	40
Tornados / My Worst Fear	41
A Bigger Boat	42
It Came Up So Quickly	43
108 Years	44
Submerged / The Parade	45
A Bigger Boat	46
Fresh / Water	47
Observation / Mt. Rainier	48
Bikini / Good Question	49
The Ocean Is In The Road	50
The Sea / Bungalow	51
Tornado / What Frightens Me The Most	52
It Added Up To Devastation	53
There Are Boats In The Street Five Blocks From The Ocean	54
The Water / Message	55
Postscript	56

For My Parents
&
Lori, Hailey & Chloe

"…and then I dreamed of clouds opening up and dropping such riches on me that when I woke up, I cried because I wanted to dream again."
~ Shakespeare, *The Tempest*, Act III, Scene ii

The Sea / Bikini

What more do you want washed out?
The sea came and covered everything like it does

A girl I knew in third grade splashing
in the water – the only one to show up

Now a woman in a red bikini offering to help
sweep the sand off the water-logged floors

The sky was gray and we saw a map of New Jersey
This water was terrible in that it covered everything
Like it does

Thoughts About Water

When I was very young
I was convinced only the surface
of the water was wet

That under the surface was
just a flowing softness

How to get to it but
through the surface and its tension?

I spent many nights awake
imagining breaking that line
and staying dry

I wish I could remember how to do it

A Bigger Boat

We were prepared with provisions and batteries. Nothing will touch us here. I told my wife that nothing would touch us here and we both told our daughter that nothing would touch us here. We eventually went to bed in the dark and while they slept I listened to something very large coming slowly over a great distance breathe down on top of us. I felt the air pressure change. There were pops and cracks and creaks and other synonyms. I did not feel dread – I felt resignation. When I was younger I was driving during a snowstorm and pulled onto the entrance ramp to the highway. My tires lost traction and I slid sideways toward the guardrail and restraining wall. I had enough time to take my hands off the wheel and cover my face as I watched it all happen. There was no time to be afraid, but there was time to think *I am going into that wall and I cannot stop it.* I assumed the crash would be horrific. It was not horrific. I went through the guardrail and bounced off the restraining wall back onto the pavement. I came to a stop on the shoulder of the road with only a cut on my neck from the seatbelt. Inevitability frightens me. Now I was in my bed slowly watching the walls shake. This is coming and I cannot stop it. I wanted to cover my face. I wanted to cover their faces. I wanted to cover everything.

When it finally came, yes Virginia, it was horrific.

Teeth

Now it is my teeth again
The left side of my lower jaw
I put a band-aid over it and it held very firm
Once a week this happens and I don't know why

Perhaps I grind them
Perhaps it is anxiety, but I am not anxious
I have made sure that I am not anxious
I have shrugged anxiety off of me like a poorly fitted hat

But I have these teeth
Their surfaces are worn flat
and cracks appear more often than I would think
They tell me it is from grinding them because of anxiety

Why should I worry just because I can see the storm before anyone else?
There are already bodies tumbling within it

My body may be tumbling within it

I Never Thought I'd See What I Saw Today

You don't understand when I say *gone*
I mean it doesn't *exist* anymore

There are many things that were once there

my hands, your mouth, etc.

I have lost all the pictures, the arcade tickets,
but I remember a motel room, a broken window,
a girl's name, her hand on my hand

Those things don't exist anymore, either

A Bigger Boat

My father was always worried about the large tree in the front yard. He was sure it would eventually fall on the house – fall through the roof and into the living room. When it came he and my mother and my brother were in the basement waiting for the water to seep up from the ground. They were prepared for the water. When the lights went out they took their flashlights and waited, checking the floor and under the door for the water that would eventually come. They weren't sure what the noise was but my father immediately thought of the tree. They ran upstairs into the living room and looked up. The roof was still there. The tree in the front yard was still there. They returned to the basement. Later that night, my brother climbed the stairs to the second floor and thought everything sounded so much louder than before. Then he smelled the water. He turned his flashlight towards the bedrooms. A tree had fallen through the roof, through the bedrooms. He could see the lightning through the hole. The water had been pouring in for hours, spreading uninterrupted over everything. It would continue to pour in unabated for hours and hours.

The Water Speaks / I Am Furious

I am furious
and I am coming
for the land
and all that rests on it

I want to take it all
inside of me
to ingest it
I will spit out

what does not interest me
but remember:
there are *many* things
that interest me

Submerged / The Water

For some reason the water has been coming frequently
I don't believe it is carrying anything out to sea like I used to

I think that now it is just bringing more and more water

Flooding the homes built over the sand, but my home
is not built over the sand

The water is coming anyway

A Bigger Boat

And the radio said you're all going to die! You laughed at the men carrying the signs all over Union Square but now the joke is on you! And the radio said Armageddon is coming in gradually increasing swells that will take what it wants and you are powerless to stop it! And the radio said start praying from now because you'll want a soul rid of lies and deceit. And the radio said you came from the loving waters of your mother's womb, and you were baptized in His name with His sacred water, and now you will be cast back to that water, back to that briny abyss from where all life came. And the radio said it's too late to build your ark, it's too late to measure out all those cubits, it's too late to round up the animals – let the poor creatures be! And the radio said the water is coming and it will wash us clean, like a cats' tongue over our unworthy skin. And the radio said we are all mostly water, and now the water will be mostly us. And the radio said look at all you've done! You will reap what you sow and you have sown tears and tears for millennia! And the radio said learn to swim, you fuckers, we are in tall buildings watching you. And the radio laughed. And the radio crackled in time with the lightning. And the radio went to static, because the water took the radio as well.

Submerged / Library

In the library they kept the books submerged in water
and when they needed to read them they dried them off

I didn't understand then but I think I do now:
We are made up mostly of water
but the books I love so much are
frightened by their need to absorb

I do not know if I am frightened by my need to absorb,
but I take all this into me and don't want to let it go

The truth is so sad it makes my teeth hurt:
Everything eventually has to be submerged
when there is this much water

A Bigger Boat

In the morning my father had laid out hundreds of old pictures, each one soggy and curling on the dining room table. We could smell the dampness of the carpets, of the walls, of the ceiling, of everything that we had thought was safe. He said *The next time you write one of those list poems where you just list a whole bunch of stuff you should write one called "Things That The Water Took." It would be pages long.* He opened all the windows, then he looked for something heavy to flatten out the photos.

Things That The Water Took

The roof, the ceiling, the beds, the floors, the walls,
my grandfather's desk in the corner of my old bedroom
filled with more of my memories than I can recall,
three Roberto Clemente rookie cards, a sword my father
carried home from Scotland, comic books I haven't read
in twenty years but always thought I might again, books
and books and books and books, my high school varsity
jacket with my name in gold stitching, a pair of light blue
Pumas that my father has had since the early '70s but I stole
from him because they looked so retro and cool,
my grandfather's papers, including his honorable discharge
and the notebooks he kept with doodles running up and down
the margins, an autobiographical doll I made in the 8th
grade from a liter bottle of soda that had my dreams of
the future sealed inside, pictures, photos, many feet deep
that will never be recognizable again, small birthday
presents from friends I no longer have, the dried corsage
from my senior prom, my high school yearbooks with their
pages filled with scribbled requests not to ever change,
pillows, blankets, a baseball signed by Hank Aaron
and my dad's high school baseball coach, a pen from
Disney World covered in mouse ears, the old answering
machine with the cassette still in it that I would record
parody outgoing messages, the notebooks with the first
drafts of everything I wrote between 1993 and 2003,
my name badge from the Christmas I worked at Macy's,
trophies, my baseball glove, Star Wars toys, a television,
old newspapers we had all deemed important enough
to keep, hundreds of figurines, a mirror from above my

old bed, the feelings of safety and security in your own home, the faulty thinking that *this doesn't happen here, that doesn't apply to us, that won't reach us, it's just water, it's just water, it's just water, it's just water, it's just water, it's just water, it's just water, it's just water, it's just water,* along with so many other things that my mind just won't allow me to force recollection of them

The Water Speaks / The Taste

The taste is something I have
had before
It smacks of late summers
early autumns

But I intend to swallow
it all now
I intend to chew it up
and leave nothing on my plate

I will lick this seaboard clean

The Bikini / The Water

The bikini may have had white polka dots; I don't remember

Her hair was in pigtails and she danced in the water

It was so strange that I recognized her after all these years
and stranger that she recognized me and offered to help

I assume the water drove everyone else away

All I can think about is the water

It Will Be Different

Every time I go back it is different
but this is a different kind of different

This is the kind of different where
you lose your bearings and nausea
climbs up your shaking body

This is the different where people say
They rebuilt Dresden after the firebombing
but they have never been to Dresden, never
saw a firebombing, didn't have their own
hair singed off their arms and faces, never
heard what a spiraling funnel of fire sounds like

This is the kind where you begin to pray
without realizing that you are praying

A Bigger Boat

In the dark, I told stories to my daughter. I told her about the times we drove to Florida, the time I drank so much orange juice that I got sick, the time her Uncle Michael rolled away down a hill, the time a giraffe looked into our hotel window. We told her we were going to *batten down the hatches*. Then I told her stories about Mighty Mouse. I tried to remember the ones my mother used to tell me but I couldn't, so I made ones up where Mighty Mouse saves a milk truck dangling over a bridge, saves a giraffe whose head was stuck in a tree. She likes giraffes. Eventually I ran out of stories. I half-heartedly sang show tunes until I no longer knew their words. I began to make things up. I talked for hours and she listened intently. The roof was shaking. I talked more. I talked until the flashlights dimmed. I talked until I was sure she was asleep. I rolled over. She opened her eyes. Then she turned and asked me what was outside; why was it trying to rip the roof off? Was it trying to come inside? Why did whatever was out there really want to come inside? I wished someone would tell me a story.

Submerged / A Small Book

You have a small book in your hands
and are travelling thousands of miles with it
and you take pictures of places you've been
including the inside of barns and art galleries

You will make a small book of your own
filled with these pictures and your thoughts
and I will read this book and remind you
of everything that is still missing

I want to buy your book and absorb it
so that even when it has left me I am
fundamentally changed – yes, still readable,
but not at all the same as before

A Bigger Boat

In the morning I went outside. Everything was destroyed. The trees were snapped like pencils and pieces of houses lay scattered throughout the street. Anything lighter than a car had been picked up and thrown. My neighbor across the street sat in a lawn chair in his driveway. He waved at me. I walked over and told him that we were leaving to find a place with electricity, or at least water and heat. He told me he would call if anything else happened to the house. I didn't know what else to say. *Enjoying the peace?* I asked. *No*, he said. He was waiting for the looters. He lifted the magazine on his lap and a .45 pistol lay on his crotch. He rubbed his beard and shook his head. *There will be no looters on this street*, he told me. I gave a half-smile. Then he became frighteningly serious and said, again, *There will be no looters on this street.*

The Water Speaks / You Can Run

You can run and hide from me
That is fine and expected
Hide in your home, your car

I will simply take your home
take your car
take it all in my ever-widening mouth

I know I will die here
so I will take one last gulp
of all that is dry and clean

Let it pass over my salty lips

I Do Not Like This

I did not wave my arms wildly enough
or this is just the way things work out

I think that this is just the way things work out
and this time there was no blood
I do not like this
I do not like this at all

Even with less blood there is more of something else
Something else is just as bad

I sat and watched a big board with your name
until it was finished at 10:17 and then the big
board told me it was finished

That's when I realized it was over
What was over?
Something else

A Bigger Boat

I weaved through the debris: trees, siding, shopping carts, glass, power lines, telephone poles. A tornado had touched down and stripped the trees of everything. It had snapped them in half ten feet above the ground in a fifty-yard stretch for more than a mile. I took side streets. The highway was flooded with water and abandoned cars. We drove north until it was obvious there was nothing there for us. I turned and went south. We passed people in front of what was left of their homes. Some were crying. They looked at us as we slowly moved by. My house was still there and I couldn't look at them. I turned the radio off and drove over front lawns when the street itself was underwater. We reached a portion of the highway that was open and I took it. The river next to it was not angry; it was incensed. It had become a grown man in a child's crib. As we passed it I saw its fingers reach over the banks onto the roadway. And then I watched as it took the road. Honest to God, the river reached up, grabbed the highway and pulled two lanes down into it. I saw cars slamming on their breaks and cutting to their left. Where the road was it was now just two hundred feet of incensed river. *Oh my God*, I said. My wife turned. *What happened?* she asked. *The river took the highway.* So help me God, it reached up and took the highway.

The Hudson River Came

I was going to tell a joke
but you're already laughing

So then I tell you the truth
only to realize that you
weren't laughing, you were
doing something else

You tell me to tell the joke
anyway, but it doesn't sound
funny anymore, in fact it is
now depressing and vulgar

You wait for a punchline
that I won't tell you

Submerged / Photo In A Barn

This is no oppressive heat—there is only a profound stickiness holding me in place like a heavy pin

I roll my eyes, then roll them again and think more of the books

A poet on a ladder looking for a friend

Inscribed copies submerged in a tank

An Art History professor noticing my shoes are too small

The books are spinning on a rack

The book I want is not here

A Bigger Boat

This was before I even knew about what else the water had taken.

Stay Pure

I will let the water cleanse me
I will stay pure in its' vacuous eye
I will watch the water break
Watch it come
Submit to its wishes
As if I have a choice of submission

Submerged / You Look Perfect

You rolled up your sleeves
in the barn and posed for a photo

You look perfect

Everyone in that barn is famous
now and has a tattoo
You spoke about getting
a tattoo with a man who has a beard
and has written many books

None of these books are about
tattoos or water or beards

An 18 year-old alone in a park
laughs at this and thinks
What else could there be?

A Bigger Boat

A man sat in his living room with his wife and son. He had a 60 foot tree lying across the roof. A newspaper photographer had already taken pictures of it for the paper. The generator was humming outside. They were keeping the baby formula cold and heating it when it was time to feed him. The radio said looters were stealing gasoline and small generators, even if they were running. They were siphoning gas from cars in driveways at night. The man sat in a chair with the front door to his left, the window overlooking the generator to his right, and a loaded handgun in his lap. He waited for days.

Submerged / Singing

In every basement there is someone singing
I know, because I've been in every basement

(but I only sang in some of them)

What few people know is that I wrote that song

I wrote that song on a diner placemat and folded
it into my wallet and left it there until the water came

Something Happened

This happens all the time
and we barely realize it

Once something happened
and I touched a girl's breast

Once something happened
and I broke my arm in half

Sometimes these things happen
Other times I spit out saltwater

Most times, though, these things
happen without us treading water

A Bigger Boat

We slept on floors and couches. We visited our house to make sure it was still okay. My neighbor was sitting in his lawn chair in his driveway. He no longer had a magazine, just a shotgun across his knees. He waved and yelled *No looters, yet.* I think he really wanted the opportunity to shoot someone. We went back to my in-laws. We waited on line for gasoline. We waited on line for fresh water. We waited for the power company. I waited with a knife on my belt because I had seen too many fistfights while waiting on lines and fistfights with people who were trying to get on line and fistfights with people who had been on line, but I was surprised at how calm and helpful most people were. My parents waited for someone to tarp where their roof once had been. They waited for someone to come and remove the tree that was lying in their bedroom and my old bedroom. They waited for someone to come and start fixing the cracks around the window frames and the ones through the ceiling where the tree did not hit but cracked them anyway. They waited for things to dry. They started going through the debris. They threw almost everything out but the photos. They slept on the floor and the couches. My daughter asked if we were going to have to *batten down the hatches* again. I told her *no.*

I See That A New Lake Has Formed

I looked out of the window
and to my surprise found
a new lake had formed

Where there were once houses
is now a lagoon with small
cresting waves battering my front stairs

I see the peak of a house
rising towards the west
and I wonder many things

You are now in a revered aquarium
and this is a poem that you will never read

Submerged / Manhattan

We took a non-existent bridge
into lower Manhattan
and went straight to the hotel
on its southern tip

The hotel was on the water
and shaped like a boat

At some point the water
began to breach it
and I thought to myself,
Water, again

A Bigger Boat

We watched the news and saw the houses that were washed out to sea, the towns that were washed out to sea, the bodies they had found in the marsh, the bodies they wouldn't find. We watched the news and saw the roller coaster in the middle of the Atlantic, the boardwalk picked up and taken away, the fires burning.

Tornados / My Worst Fear

My worst fear is tornados
I dream of them frequently
They are often very far away
but I can see them on the horizon

I find this even more frightening
than if they were right outside
my door blowing in my windows
and ripping off my second floor

because there is the possibility
they will blow in my windows
and rip off my second floor and
possibility is the scariest thing of all

A Bigger Boat

Mantoloking, Belmar, Ortley Beach, the difference between Seaside Heights and Seaside Park, the difference between Casino Pier and Funtown Pier, Moonachie, Little Ferry, Oyster Creek Nuclear Generating Station, Lavalette, Bayonne, Hoboken, Jersey City, Point Pleasant, Barnegat Light, Ship Bottom, Long Beach, Bay Head, Beach Haven, Sandy Hook, Atlantic City, 346,000 homes, 2.4 million households, 37 people.

The names were read like a roll call. The names were flashed on the television. The names scrolled across the bottom of the screen for days and days and days. They repeated like a mantra.

There's nothing left for me.

It Came Up So Quickly

This was the punchline to the joke
that I wouldn't tell you

Of course you'd laugh, now
We are all drunk with love

We are drunk with entire towns
being carried away in the current

I am drunk with thoughts
that I cannot stop thinking

108 Years

In 108 years we had never faced anything
like what we faced

Subways flooded, garages consumed

But the people – the people –

Especially the ones found in the marshlands
swept away like breadcrumbs

To be left where the ocean now meets the land

Submerged / The Parade

There was a parade and much activity proceeding
down a cross street and I looked immediately for a bathroom

The water would wash this all away, I'm sure
and everything looks like a jigsaw puzzle to me

Sometimes I cannot believe how easily
the floor gave way beneath us

A Bigger Boat

I know in other places millions of people were swept out to sea, but I did not see that. This is what I saw.

Fresh / Water

I always picture the water as fresh water
It is so clear and looks so refreshing

Part of me wants to force my head under
and take long gulps until I have no thirst

Then I realize: Yes, that will be the way it ends

Observation / Mt. Rainier

We watched it from a distance, me and you
We prefer watching everything from a distance

It was 2,838 miles away and we stood
on the Palisades to see the small flash

You know what it was but I'm not sure
It was dark and there were animals

This has nothing to do with the water
just long distances and our keen eye

You ask if this was in a dream I had
My dreams have more detail than this

I am frightened that this was real
I am frightened of these real things

You assure me it never happened
Then I think it is only a distraction

It had me facing west, and we all know
the water is coming from the east

Bikini / Good Question

The girl in the red polka-dot bikini is waiting for me
She is not wearing her bikini, she is wearing something else

She is sitting in a diner in my hometown
planning our high school reunion
She is waiting for me to return

I have never left, I will tell her
But where have you been? she will say

That is a good question

I have been slowly building myself
committing quiet repairs that I don't talk about

I have been having prophetic dreams of water

She will give me a list of old classmates who have died
I will not read it

The water will take everyone anyway

The Ocean Is In The Road

Most shark attacks occur
ten feet from shore

But now the ocean is in the road

No one expects a shark attack
ten feet from their front door

Then again, you never expected
the ocean to be in the road

Yet here it is climbing the front
steps your grandfather built

You want to turn and say
You're gonna need a bigger house

Oh, darling, there's no one there
They've all paddled off down the street

The Sea / Bungalow

As a child each summer we would rent a bungalow on the boardwalk
We would sit on the porch at night and watch the ships' lights

When I would go to sleep I would have many dreams of the horizon,
of the sea receding and then rushing back in over us

I cut my finger in the kitchen and worried about infections
I worried about sunburn and many things

One summer the heat melted the tracks of the tiny train running
up and down the boardwalk, from the bungalows to the arcade

I was so young and already I was aware of the water, in appropriate awe

It would not leave us clean

I wanted to go home
Everything comes from the water, it said

I stuck a piece of driftwood into the sand, drew my line

Tornado / What Frightens Me The Most

I rarely dream of driving in the snow
More often I dream of hiding from
tornados that may strike at any moment

But there are no tornados here, you say

And that is what frightens me the most:
you would never expect them to show up

And that is what frightens me the most:
they only look for the most unsuspecting

And that is what frightens me the most:
eventually I will put my guard down

And that is what frightens me the most:
when it came I was sleeping in a warm bed

It Added Up To Devastation

When it is all added
it seems to be more
indicative of subtraction
but I am not a math major

Perhaps adding negative
numbers makes sense
but we started positive
from what I remember

There Are Boats In The Street Five Blocks From The Ocean

What we were dealing with
is a perfect engine, a machine
that swallows everything
whole and leaves nothing behind

All this machine does is flood
the land, eat houses, highways,
trees, entire neighborhoods,
spits out splinters of boardwalks

It carries boats to streets
five blocks from the ocean
and never turns to look back,
leaving us to turn and look back

The Water / Message

For generations my family was seafaring

They captained large wooden boats
and put down mutinies
and pissed into the green sea

For one hundred years the sea held its tongue
Now I know this:
That water carried a spiteful message

I listened intently to the foam
until I could make out its salted voice:

You can be anything you want
but you know that I am hungry
and I will fucking eat you whole

Postscript

The trees are still bare where the winds ripped through
shredded and bare –

still lying down where they were bent over
snapped and circular now

Homes have been rebuilt and the bodies all buried

but we still have nightmares of the water rising unabated
the wind reaching down and taking what it wanted

highways disappearing, the bodies floating off

the stories we told, fading – fading

This is why we write to remember

www.ingramcontent.com/pod-product-compliance
Lightning Source LLC
Chambersburg PA
CBHW070104120526
44588CB00034B/2269